In SJ Sindu's extraordinary new chapbook, her speaker lives in a world in which women are punished for their pleasure, rage, and attempts at freedom. Exploring ancient stories, like the *Mahabharata*, as well as the speaker's own experiences growing up as a queer person in Sri Lanka and the US, *Dominant Genes* pulls at the strings that have stitched together our identities, making clear the social and cultural constraints that limit the freedom of women and gender nonconforming people. With tenderness and compassion toward her family, this smart, unflinching collection envisions a life for the speaker in which she does not inherit misogyny or her mother's idea of progress, a life in which she is the "seed in her own fruit."

—MARIANNE CHAN,
author of *All Heathens*

"I want to inherit your anger, and use your story to stitch my two selves back together," writes SJ Sindu in this hybrid collection, poems and lyric essays weaving together the fragments of a life bifurcated across racial, familial, and queer identities. Blurring both genre and gender, Sindu questions descendancy, dominant genes something to unspool, silence something to unstitch, rage a means of survival. Yet as this collection undoes Sri Lankan matrilineal expectation, pulling at the faithless thread of what it means to inherit a story that does not serve you, it spins a richer myth of legacy and self, one that pierces like a needle.

—SARAH FAWN MONTGOMERY,
author of *Quite Mad*

The most thrilling feature of SJ Sindu's *Dominant Genes* is its distinctive, multifaceted probing of *expectation*: the dynamic, often devastating, gap between what we hope for and what we live with. Sindu's explorations of historical, societal, parental, and personal expectations—those tense and fertile convergences of duty, possibility, inevitability, and desire—yield piercing flashes of wonder, anger, insight, and joy. In her daring, masterful, genre-expanding work, Sindu enlivens and expands our expectations for what a collection can be and how writing can reveal, provoke, and inspire.

—DANIEL SCOTT TYSDAL,
author of *Wave Forms and Doom Scrolls*, *Fauxccasional Poems*,
and *The Mourner's Book of Albums*

DOMINANT GENES

DOMINANT GENES

SJ SINDU

BLACK LAWRENCE PRESS

 Black
Lawrence
Press

www.blacklawrence.com

Executive Editor: Diane Goettel
Chapbook Editor: Kit Frick
Book and Cover Design: Zoe Norvell

Published 2022 by Black Lawrence Press.
Printed in the United States.

Contents

Birth Story

My mother, out of love, stitches up my heart, pulling the thread tight to make sure it won't rupture again at the same spot. My heart is defenseless, ready to come undone at the next crisis. While she's at it, my mother stitches up my mouth, too, and turns her needle and thread to my brain.

Gods in the Surf

I envy my American city friends
their impractical swimsuits
made to be seen not touched by sea
unable to stand in weak Florida surf
I was born by the ocean an island child
the core of me salt water and seagulls howling
we wade into the Gulf the ocean holds us
amniotic fluid shot with jumping mullets
jellyfish constellations too small to see
worming their stinging tendrils into skin
waves spitting shark eggs and tangles of seaweed
pelicans strafe the water we gorge on chips
chug shitty beer under a rainbow umbrella
my city friends tell stories innocent childhood
beach trips Florida vacations coconut sunscreen
back home people saw gods in the surf
watery limbs and hair made of dirty foam
fishermen went out to sea came back
nets full of prawns to bombed out homes
children tried to hide in the sand
evading military planes only to shatter on land mines
I never saw visions in the waves but I knew
a boat with no motor and no lights
could take me across a lagoon at night
and if I heard a helicopter
I should sink my body into the ocean
and trust it to hold me

Draupadi Walks Alone at Night

For years now, since I turned twenty, my parents have been trying to marry me off. Aunties cup my chin at parties, turn my head this way and that, and say things like, "she's so fair, too bad she's short," and, "she could use a thicker head of hair, but she's pretty, so it'll balance out." My worth measured in pigments and strands. Point: I look younger than I am. Point: I'm neither skinny nor fat. Point: I come from a dominant caste.

Someone in a Bollywood picture says that progress is when a woman decked in gold can walk alone down the street at night. Of course, a film version of civility would include 22-karat bangles and jumka earrings. In the movie, a woman tries it. Police freak out. Comedy ensues. Centuries of feminine rage unspool on celluloid.

This is a rage we've all inherited, folded up in the pleats of cotton sarees, transmuted from the heads of our mothers at the same time they scolded us for not knowing how to cook roti, and how will we keep a man happy? We learn our anger through osmosis, or maybe it's in the breast milk, spreading through our veins long before we learn how to look only at the floor and walk without showing our ankles.

In rural India, women are still married off to their rapists, a practice considered both a punishment for the rapist and justice for the woman.

My own insides curdle with this anger. I cut off my hair, hoping the outrage will seep out through my scalp, but it lingers.

In the *Mahabharata*, Draupadi marries five brothers and bears their children, rules as queen and eventually, ends up suffering in exile. For all that, she is called a whore. A queen, and for all that, a man can still gamble her away, a man can still drag her out to the middle of a crowd and order her stripped, a man can still save her body from shame.

Every time I go back home, my mother tells me what to pack. *Bring shorts, but not too short, mid-thigh to knee, and for gods' sake make sure you bought them from the women's section. If you bring men's tank tops, I swear I will burn them all.* My mother has a problem with androgyny.

By the time I'm twenty, I identify as a lesbian. I've cut my hair. I've bought twice as many men's tank tops. And the boy I bring home to my mother still has the girl body he was born with. My little brother, who is eight, is not confused. My mother cries. My father is stone.

Draupadi spends the first year of her marriage with the oldest brother, the second year with the second oldest, and so on. This so that everyone will know which son belongs to which father. She is the lynchpin of the story, a victim of masculine sexuality like Sita of the *Ramayana*. The narrative revolves around her, but unlike Sita, no parents today name their daughters Draupadi. Sita the virgin and Draupadi the whore.

The questions are simple. But no one asks them. No one wants answers. No one even wants the questions. The questions are landfills that loom like mountains.

I tell my mother I'm bisexual. Bi, from the Latin *dui*, the Greek *di*, the Sanskrit *dvi*. Meaning double. Having two. Living in two. I have bifurcated: my life, brown and white; my family, my parents and me; my body, masculine and feminine. Bi, meaning two. Draupadi, the wife and the whore. Bi, meaning co-existence, meaning contradiction, meaning war.

4

I spend years meeting potential suitors who are arranged by my parents. I don't think they'll work out, but I want to keep my parents from the breaking point. My mother calls to say that I'm not trying hard enough, and why can't I just be a good daughter and make them happy?

One suitor asks me to cook for him, watches me as I make curried beets, assures me that he can handle the spice I dump in. He can't.

Later, in a bar, a drunk white man asks us when we are getting married. *You both have good teeth*, he says, *and you're both from the Hindu Kush, so why wouldn't you marry each other?* Because I like women. Because my white boyfriend is holding empty my space in his bed, wondering when I'll come home. I can tell the drunk man that I will marry this suitor and make my parents happy, but that would be a lie.

Before Draupadi is a mother, she is a wife, and before she is a wife, she is a daughter, begotten through prayer from the fire god Agni. A princess so otherworldly that only a man who can shoot a fish in the eye can have her. But she is still a woman, and so she is an object, a prize to be won and a prize to be shared.

As I near thirty, my parents grow more desperate. They consult astrologists, cross-check with priests and mystics expert in past lives. They learn that I was a landowner named Indrani who treated her workers poorly and was doomed to pay for it in the next life. She didn't allow her female workers to take time off to be with their husbands, and so my married life will be rocky.

My mother prays for me, fasts for me, chants the Lord's 108 names every day for me. She says the chanting is supposed to help with her own anger, too. All I can tell is that my rebellion has numbed her, and I've inherited her anger.

Some say Draupadi got what was coming to her, because she had insulted kings and scoffed at their bids for her hand. She laughed at one king when he fell, *the blind son of blind parents*, she had said. Of another king, she had said, *I will not marry a man of unknown parentage.* So they called her a whore. They wanted her bared naked in front of her court. They wanted her fallen. And still some say they loved her.

You're going to end up alone, my mother tells me. *It's because of your anger. Your anger pushes men away.*

When Draupadi's mother-in-law mistakenly orders her sons to share the prize they've won, Draupadi becomes angry and tries to leave. What if she *had* left? She could have married one man and been happy. She could have married many men. She could have still been queen. At least it would have been her choice.

I come out to my mother three times. Each time she consoles me, sits by me while I cry, strokes my hair and tells me that I can still marry a man and have children, that I don't have to be different. Bi, meaning two paths. One path lets me stay in their lives. The other sees me cast out. My mother tells me to choose.

Lord Krishna explains to Draupadi that in her past life, she asked for a husband with five qualities. And since no perfect man exists, she got five husbands. In the end, it's all still her fault, and still not her choice. In the end, she gets no choices. In the end, she swallows her anger, marries the men and becomes a devoted wife, which my mother would say is a good choice.

At my cousin's wedding, everyone tells me I'm next. *The stars are lining up*, they say. *You'll be married within the year*, they say. No one seems to be worried that I'm still single. They're hoping the next suitor will work out.

At a coffee shop after the bar, I tell the next suitor about my bisexuality, my polyamory, my plans to not have children. He blinks, sips at his latte, avoids eye contact. *You didn't have to tell me that*, he says. *You could have hidden that from me. You'll have to hide it from everyone if we get married.* I drink my coffee to keep the anger down.

My therapist is worried about my health. *Have you had suicidal ideation? This world needs you.* My boyfriend is tiring of my anger. This rage sits between us, grates against our skins like sand pressed too hard. I contemplate being alone. If Draupadi had given in to her anger and walked away, she might have died alone. That's the kind of story my mother would use to scare me into obedience.

Progress—like a woman's worth—is not measured in gold. It's not measured in gossip, eyelashes, or honor. Progress is the ways in which our gendered roles have blended and blurred. My mother went to grad school. My father cooks half the nights. My brother grew up in day care. But my mother says that we've had enough. She says, *further progress will unravel us.*

Draupadi, I want to rewrite your story. I want you to walk away. I want you to get world-shakingly mad. I want your rage to cut through everything and spin the world into new string. I want to use that string to bind my mother's idea of progress to mine, to weave my own rage into an armor, to wrap up tired old gender ideas and burn them in effigy. Draupadi, I want to inherit your anger and use your string to stitch my two selves back together.

Pant Hoot

after Andrew Westoll's *The Chimps of Fauna Sanctuary*

yesterday a man
visited my class
taught us all
how to laugh
like chimpanzees
together we vocalized

hou—hou—hou—hou—

invoking survivor chimps
in a sanctuary
outside Montreal
I wanted to know
how often they laugh

chimps freed from labs
cut open every week
shot up with tranquilizers
injected with HIV
housed in floating cages

Rachel the saved chimp
has episodes she chews
on herself bites
her own fingers bloody
only last week I lay in bed

screaming and hitting
myself in the face
until my partner spread
his body out over mine
like a gravity blanket

in middle school I poked
my wrists with needles
planting seeds or venting steam
surviving doesn't always mean
you're healed

when they're not ramming
shoulders into cage bars
or spinning themselves
in endless stress circles
the chimps laugh

hou—hou—hou—hou—

My Parents Crossed an Ocean
and Lost Me

I carved myself a new face. They searched and searched, and found God instead.

They built an altar for God in the office room closet. Sliding doors, LED lights, images of God in all his iterations—Vishnu, Parvati, Shiva, Murugan, even a tiny portrait of Jesus and a bottle of holy water shaped like the Virgin Mary, so as not to leave out the God of their new country.

My parents took to God like they took to America, like they took to money locked in savings accounts. We used to be penniless, stateless, godless. Like money, like country, God was a newish something.

My mother now spends her days praying. She and God have a thing. My father roams the empty rooms, fills them with the voices of angry white pundits on TV.

When I visit, we fight—God and I—for my parents' affection. We're siblings born too far apart in age to be friends.

Sun God

In the *Mahabharata* Karna the infant
is set afloat in a basket

illegitimate son of a princess
and the sun, raised by a merchant

his real story is one of self-destruction
I try to be an expert on this subject

Karna grows up to be an archer
the finest in the world

until his little half-brother
comes along to best him

Karna finally makes a friend
just his luck it's the villain of our tale

and now he's on the wrong side of a holy war
all the gods get involved

even his mother comes to him
the mother he yearns for

but now she's come and revealed herself
only to ask him not to kill his half-brother

Karna is no Moses
and he will have no redemption

no hordes of followers
no one to pray over him

no, he will be a symbol
of how even the sun will abandon us

of how the wrong birth
is deserving of pity but not hero-hood

and how exactly did the sun
get a woman pregnant

is what I want to know
I'm told this is a bad question

I'm full of bad questions
like if I peel open my labia in the light

will I too have to send away a child
in a basket on the river

and what about masturbation
was the princess being punished

for digging inside herself
for her own deep pleasure

why can't women step inside the temple
when they're bleeding

I imagine little Karna sits at breakfast
while his adoptive mother stirs the sambar

and he is full of bad questions like
if you're my real mother

then why do I feel like a god
and what I wanted to know at his age

was if one man's freedom fighter
is another man's terrorist

then are we on the wrong side of this war
but this a bad question

Parental Love

When I tell my parents I'm depressed, my mother, like a good Asian, doesn't believe me. She chalks it up to weakness of character, stress, overwork. My father says nothing, but afterward makes my favorite fish head curry.

Silently he feeds me all my favorite foods. He reminds me to watch TV, to relax. He asks me if I need money, tells me to treat myself to theater tickets, and sends me overnight packages of his cooking packed into little air-sealed frozen baggies.

I stack the bags, now soft and melting, into my freezer. These could feed me for months, if I ration them out, but I eat them ravenously, for every meal, holding off the anxiety with each bite.

When the food is gone, the storm inside me sparks back to life, and I wait for my next shipment.

Girls from the Island

at Christmas with my family
we scan our faces through an app
to see what we'll look like in ten
twenty, forty years

I'll look like my mother
then like her mother
sagging caramel face
slowly bleaching white
like driftwood
left too long on a beach

inescapable:
a bird's foot
caught in its own nest

women in my family never die
if only from stubbornness

later during quarantine
my grandmother calls with ideas
she's been talking to someone
who heard from someone
whose friend knows ayurvedic medicine

here are four ways
to keep disease at bay
no global pandemic
can penetrate the sheer will
of my grandmother's wishing

under her direction
my pregnant cousin
strings beads of dried asafetida gum
into a necklace and wears it
to her pre-natal appointment

Grandmother makes all us cousins
promise to mix equal parts
red rice flour, white flour,
and turmeric with water
sculpt a diya lamp
the size of an open palm
fill it with oil
place it in our doorways
and the virus will burn from our faith

she tells me, cut up an onion
and keep the pieces around the house
boil a fistful of dried red chili peppers
with tablets of camphor
until smoke fills you

the British ended matriarchy in Sri Lanka
but only on paper

even across the water in India
they tell young grooms
not to marry a girl from the island

my grandmother gave me
bad knees and panic attacks
when my grandfather had a stroke
my grandmother thought
she was having one too
her fingers turned icicle
her heart broke her chest open
the world held no air

my grandmother
thought she would die with him
this mindset is what I've inherited
along with her female-pattern baldness

but I've resisted whatever gene
makes her believe a flower garland
draped across a god's picture in a gilded frame
will grow if you pray hard enough
and a Ganesh statue
in some temple across the world
is drinking the milk offered by devotees

this, my grandmother tells me
is true faith
this, her legacy

Banana Tree Wedding

My parents consult an astrologer about my future. The stars say that I will be married twice. Disappointed and alarmed, my parents discuss with the astrologer, who is an expert on circumventing fate.

When I'm home for Christmas break, my parents ask me to go to temple. I normally wouldn't wear a saree, but they insist. They take me to a temple that's housed in a strip mall behind the dentist's office where I had my wisdom teeth removed years before.

At the threshold, we take off our shoes to show respect to the gods. No one else is here so early on a Saturday. According to the sign posted at the entrance, the temple is closed, but the door is unlocked, and we let ourselves in.

Inside, the temple is dark and carpeted. On the altar, an eight-by-eight-foot square of blankets holds brass lamps, copper jugs of grains, a fire pit, a bearded coconut wearing a skirt of mango leaves, and so large an array of flowers that I can't even name them all. It's a wedding ceremony. My wedding ceremony.

The priest arrives with his six-year-old son, who sits in a corner with his Game Boy and doesn't look up again until we leave. The priest drags out a potted, two-foot-tall banana tree from the closet, a young sapling that fans out its three leaves to the chilly air. At my confused look, the priest says, "This is going to be your new husband."

Two hours later, the wedding ceremony reaches its climax. Traditionally, the groom ties a golden thread around the bride's neck as a necklace. But the banana tree is a tree, so instead my father offers me the necklace and asks me to tie it around the tree. I almost refuse, but then I think, when else am I going to get to be the groom? So I do it, I tie the golden thread around the stem of the tree. And we're married.

After the ceremony concludes, my father hands me a machete. And I kill my first husband, the poor little sapling, who will now never know the coziness of topsoil. The tree won't go down in one blow, so I hack at it, again and again, hitting just below the golden necklace, the trunk's fibers splitting open and leaking sap. I'm a murderer, and a widow. My parents sigh their collective relief.

That night, hushed phone conversations happen all over the world, as my family spreads the news that we've tricked the stars.

To All My Suitors and the Aunties
Who Send Them My Way

when I was young my family kept two ducks and a goat in
the backyard to give me duck eggs and goat's milk for breakfast.
now they ask me to accept a balding accountant, his body doughy
his politics centrist

I had chicken pox at nine months old and my aunts and uncles
took turns fanning the sores with bundles of curry leaves so I
wouldn't be tempted to scratch. now they ask me to marry a man who
expects me to cook for him on our first date

when I say I don't want an arranged marriage they say it's not
an arranged marriage if we date for a few months first

my aunties pass my photos and details around the globe, my eligibility
stored in the cloud. they learn gmail just so they can matchmake
by which they mean find me a boy who looks like their husbands
a boy who prays who keeps it in the caste and they say it's my
decision but not if my decision is no

in order to craft a wife who puts her husband first you have to
convince her she's not the seed in her own fruit

as a toddler at temple prayer meetings I pretended to be a radio
and I belted out Bollywood songs and when they tweaked my ear
and told me they'd turned off the radio I twisted it again
and turned myself on

Girl Next Door

I'm six. The kids next door are siblings, the boy a few months younger than me and the girl a year older. When we watch Keanu Reeves and Sandra Bullock make out in *Speed*, the girl drags me to a broom closet to teach me how it's done. After school, while their parents are out, I sneak over to their house. We pull the shutters closed, and inside the darkened rooms, we undress each other, the three of us. We squint to see our brown bodies in the afternoon shadows. We fit our nakednesses together, like puzzle pieces, and lie in each other's arms, unmoving, on a bamboo mat that covers the cement floor. That's all we do, because we think that's how it's done.

When I'm twenty and drunk, an older lesbian tells me on one of our dates that hypersexual children often have histories of sexual trauma inflicted by family or family friends. I think of the boy and the girl, how quickly they suggested our secret play. But at six years old, our afternoons are magic.

One day I invite my younger cousin, who is the boy's age, to join our secret. A single strip of light cuts across the darkened wall, and we position my cousin against it, so we can see, undressing her slowly. We get all the way to her underwear. When the girl pulls at the lace trimming of pale coral panties, my cousin gets nervous and runs home to tell on us. I act ashamed and take my scolding, but I still go back, and we make sure to play hopscotch loudly in the front yard before and after we slip away into the shadowy folds of the house.

How to Survive a Pandemic

the plague comes, the plague grows
we stop going outside
and call it social responsibility
as if we need a reason not to see each other

as if we're not already only seeing each other
through the pixels of a screen

glued to it like babes on a tit
or drunks at the bottle
is that drunk me?
maybe that drunk

is me
self-isolation, self-medication
same thing, really
lots to escape from in quarantine
lots to escape to

before puberty twisted my body
warped my skin
I was everything they wanted
I looked like a doll
the kind that closes and opens its eyes
my skin a perfect translucent honey
now, I slather on creams, dab serums, pat acids

sleep in sheet masks
trying to crawl back into my doll skin
when they told me
I was perfect

as a child I cut all the hair off my donated Barbies
the free ones I found at the laundromat
or bought for two dollars at yard sales
three-for-five deals
discarded Barbies
grimy skin and decades-out-of-fashion clothing
I snipped their shining blonde hair with safety scissors
combed Elmer's glue through the strands
styling each one into a permanent
dyke
pompadour

every time we fled the house
we left my toys behind
we moved, and moved
and moved again

as an adult, letting go is my superpower
to trash my most prized things
even as my parents hoard my old toys in their basement
this one doll gathers dust on top of the armoire:

Christmas Barbie, 1997
there's one going on Ebay for six hundred dollars

when I was seventeen at the mall
a middle-aged man told me I was perfect
like a doll and had I ever posed for photographs before
he just happened to be a photographer looking for models

his skin was inflamed from the dry Nebraska winter
little red patches peeling off his cheeks
his hands jittery in his pockets

he had me cornered in a Yankee Candle
my back against the shelves
the smell of cinnamon pine all around us

Canada and California are on lockdown
and somehow spring breakers are partying all over Florida
here, we feel full of purpose, self-righteous
yes, we're the saviors here
we're stopping a plague just by lying back

an older lesbian on YouTube
calls us pillow queens
the femmes who like to lie back
and just get done
I often disclose this tendency to potential partners
before we get into it, a warning
and to avoid embarrassment
the other word is power bottom
we're all power bottoms now

plastic cocks in a drawer
are so much better than a real one
how awful when it's attached
and I just think masculinity is so much better
served removable
when you can boil it clean

in Sri Lanka during the days of the war
there were no dolls in our house
an uncle of mine brought back
a doll from the capital
smuggled it wrapped in his lunch of rice and pickle
my grandmother washed the smell out of her hair
she was perfect and blonde
though her plastic yogurt-colored legs were hollow
not filled through like a real Barbie

I squished her legs and watched them fill back up
the plastic returning to the shape it knew
how to be

this makes me very good at quarantine
I'm good at being poor and bored

isolation was not something we got to choose

I used to love movies about dolls coming to life
and having to reckon with this world
they're the perfect outsiders
to show us our absurdity in a comforting package

made in our own image
though I never had a doll that looked like me
and I can't help but wonder if I did
whether as a teenager I would've slathered Nair all over my arms
until the lotion burned off not only my hair
but also five layers of skin
third degree chemical burns
just to look plastic and new

remember
when we left our skins
for the tingle of electric being

floating

ad infinitum in the cloud
finally reduced to our likes and timelines
finally immortal electrons?

these were the happy days
before the plague
and then after

it was out of necessity
is what we tell ourselves
giving up our skin
was the only way we knew
how to stay inside
and still be human

Self-Help

I wrote a poem
folded it like a pair
of wings
sent it to myself
in the fibrous belly of a jackfruit

All it said
was please

be happy

Mother

My mother tells me to be careful. I'm twelve years old, and we've just moved to a city outside of Boston. We live in an apartment complex that my white fiancé will call "shit housing" twenty years later when we visit. I walk to school every day, a two-mile stroll along a busy road, and my mother tells me to be careful. What she means is, keep your head down, keep walking, don't talk to anyone, I'm sorry.

I'm fifteen and my adolescent terrified-rabbit face is shifting into something that draws glances from older men. Their heads turn to watch me, and though I don't notice, though I'm deep in my teenage myopia and just want my mother and the men to leave me alone, she sees them and tells me to be careful. What she means is, the world is cruel to women, watch your back.

I'm twenty and I tell my mother I'm in love with a woman I met at my university's queer student group. My mother is silent on the phone, then tells me it's a phase everyone goes through, and don't I know what happens in the girls-only schools back home in Sri Lanka? Everyone does it, but I'll get over it. She tells me to be careful. What she means is, this isn't real love.

At twenty-seven I start dating an older white man, and my mother is begrudgingly happy. Better a man than a woman. Better cis than trans. Better straight than queer. Better older than younger. Better white than black. Her prayers have been answered. But she tells me to be careful. What she means is, don't get pregnant.

At thirty I'm married, and my ovaries are growing cysts that burst in sharp pain. I need to take hormones to control them, and my partner and I decide to never have kids. My mother tells me to be careful. What she means is, too many hormones could damage her grandchildren.

At fifty-nine my mother falls down the stairs and dislocates her shoulder. Her ligaments are floating free inside her, snapped as one bone popped itself out of its socket. She needs surgery, physical therapy, and two years of healing. I call her to tell her to be careful. What I mean is, I can't understand the fragility of your body. What I mean is, will I become soft and breakable too? What I mean is, don't leave me.

Dominant Genes

from the wombs of true believers
I came out faithless
a godless decadent heathen

but somewhere in my foggy
ancestral memory
I recall that women
used to worship snakes
we'd put out milk for cobras
hoping they'd leave the baby
in the crib alone
and if they drank from our offering
we were guaranteed
good luck for a week

but that was long ago
before the Eve-hating white men
came with injections of snake fear
shot right into our pagan faith

now when we see a cobra
we scream
and the neighbors run over
with hoes and machetes

one time when I was little
I saw one the size of my arm
slithering on our veranda
and I got to scream
cobra! cobra! snake!

they all came
men yelling to save me
my grandfather
wielding a kitchen knife
and hacking the cobra to bits
right there
in our backyard garden

my mother's mother's mother
lived to be one hundred
insisted on sleeping in her own house
until the very end

but my mother
is afraid of snakes
and as a child
tormenting her
was a favorite pastime
I'd beg snake toys from relatives
and chase her
I'd twist snakes
out of newspapers and old scarves
watching my mother
scream and run away

I laughed
I know now that it's a phobia
that she had no control
over her reaction
but back then her revulsion
was a sign of weakness
and I could feel like the strong one

I've always had a serpent tongue
though I learned early
to silence its bite
this, too, is a gift
from the women
of my family
I can cut
through a lover's blood
during any fight
this is a liability
this ability to destroy a person

when I told my mother
I wanted to be a writer
she said nothing
she didn't have to

we come from a country
where writer means *dead child*

in Harry Potter
speaking serpent tongue

meant you were evil
but really I think J.K. Rowling
couldn't imagine herself
out of her Christianity-addled brain
like how Ray Bradbury
could think up LCD wall TVs
but not a world
in which women had careers

my mother tells me
to write nice stories
to keep my serpent tongue caged
this is her wisdom
in this new world
my ancestral power
is to be feared

I'm young and I ignore her
but she still goes to sleep
every night thinking
dead child dead child dead child

Acknowledgments

Thank you to my editor, Kit Frick, and the whole team at Black Lawrence Press, for bringing this book to life.

Thank you to my professors, for everything you've taught me: Amelia Montes, Tim Schaffert, Joy Castro, Mark Winegardner, Elizabeth Stuckey-French, Skip Horack, and Barry Faulk. Thank you to my students, who teach me how to love writing every day, and especially to Noah Farberman, for helping me launch this book.

Thank you to my writing group, for all your feedback and unconditional support—Karen Tucker, Colleen Mayo, and Laurel Lathrop.

Thank you to my friends for the joy you bring to my life: Scott Schneider, Ev Evnen, Heather Bailey, Rita Mookerjee, Amy & Chris Micheals, Rob Stephens, Marianne Chan, Clancy McGilligan, Daniel Tysdal, Andrea Charise, Andrew Westoll, Jeff Boase, and Rini Kasinathan. Thank you especially to Sam Majumder, for your consistent love.

Thank you to my family—Amma, Appa, Linda, Jeff, and Courtenay. Thank you also to my aunties, uncles, and cousins, especially Ishy, Athish, and Rishana, for your love. Thank you to my brother Varun, for being a light in my world.

Thank you to Geoff Bouvier, my partner in life and in writing, for everything.

Thank you to the editors of the following publications who first published work from *Dominant Genes*:

"Banana Tree Wedding" appeared in *The Texas Review*

"Dominant Genes" appeared in *Honey Literary*

"Gods in the Surf" appeared in *Burrow Press Fantastic Floridas*

"Draupadi Walks Alone At Night" appeared in *Good Girls Marry Doctors: South Asian Daughters on Obedience and Rebellion* (Aunt Lute Books)

"My Parents Crossed an Ocean and Lost Me" appeared in *Mouths to Feed*

"To All My Suitors and the Aunties Who Send Them My Way" appeared in *ARC*

"Mother" appeared in *Cincinnati Review*

"How to Survive a Pandemic" appeared in *Prairie Schooner*

"Sun God" and "Pant Hoot" appeared in *The Bombay Review*

Land Acknowledgement

At this book's publication, I reside on the traditional lands of many nations including the Missisaugas of the Credit, the Anishnabeg, the Chippewa, the Haudenosaunee, and the Wendat peoples, which is now home to many diverse First Nations, Inuit, and Métis peoples, in the Tkaronto territory that is governed by the Dish with One Spoon wampum belt covenant.

Please read and support Indigenous authors, such as Kateri Akiwenzie-Damm, Kenzie Allen, Cherie Dimaline, Louise Erdrich, Brandon Hobson, Randy Lundy, Tommy Orange, and Tommy Pico, among others. I also urge all of us to learn more about the histories of the lands on which we live and work, including the traditional Indigenous stewards of these lands. We need to ensure that land acknowledgements such as this one are not just empty gestures but are supported by meaningful actions toward justice and peace for Indigenous peoples, and toward forging healthy relationships between the land and those who call it home.

Thank you to Kateri Akiwenzie-Damm and Randy Lundy for their advice and guidance in writing this land acknowledgement.

SJ SINDU is a Tamil diaspora author of two literary novels, two hybrid chapbooks, and a forthcoming graphic novel. Her first novel, *Marriage of a Thousand Lies*, won the Publishing Triangle Edmund White Award and was a Stonewall Honor Book and a finalist for a Lambda Literary Award. Sindu's second novel, *Blue-Skinned Gods*, was published in November 2021 by Soho Press, and her graphic novel, *Shakti*, is forthcoming from Harper Collins. Sindu's hybrid fiction and nonfiction chapbook, *I Once Met You But You Were Dead*, won the Turnbuckle Chapbook contest and was published by Split/ Lip Press. A 2013 Lambda Literary Fellow, Sindu holds an MA in English from the University of Nebraska-Lincoln and a PhD in